Beyond Thorns

Beyond Thorns

Poems

Mohineet Kaur Boparai

RESOURCE *Publications* • Eugene, Oregon

BEYOND THORNS
Poems

Resource Publications
An Imprint of Wipf and Stock Publishers
199 W. 8th Ave., Suite 3
Eugene, OR 97401

www.wipfandstock.com

PAPERBACK ISBN: 978-1-6667-4944-1
HARDCOVER ISBN: 978-1-6667-4945-8
EBOOK ISBN: 978-1-6667-4946-5

JULY 18, 2022 11:51 AM

for,
Amrit and Himmat

Hearts of the same beat

Contents

LOVE

THOUGHTS, in POETRY

Preface

Poetry as an art unravels nature and acts like a catalyst to initiate its impending blossoming in the living heart. The universal appeal of poetry springs from its infusion of beauty into the ordinary. Poetry is the synaptic space through which nature approaches and is imbibed by the being. A poem is a song that renders in words and music, the truth and beauty of nature. Poetry brings to light things and events like sunrises, violet-coloured drinks, magical seas, death and the everyday rehearsals of ordinary life, weightlessly riding on the breath of words. Poetry, like all good art, arrives effortlessly like an exhaled breath. This is not to say that a poem is nothing but an unconscious blabber and this is only indicative of the poem's tempo. There are places where a poem has been before its transliteration on the page. This experience, however, is not only immediate but radiates from an instinctive space in our being. Along with our pre-historic ancestors, poetry has trodden over the Rocky Mountains, and waded through grasslands and rippling rivers and only comes to us through a space in the mind that looks over the present through the telescope of the past.

A poem is the culmination of our links to nature and the universe. It is an avowal of the unknown, and an acceptance of the fact that we cannot know the universe in its totality, except through the experience of the elements. Poetry comes from an experience of nature, from being open to its message. A poem is a prayer, a conversation with God that transpires not through moksha, and abstinence but from experience. The universe inspires not absence of pleasure but a blissful engagement with experiencing the beauty and truth of nature. True nirvana is always born from experience of beauty and not an absence of it. Perhaps, to attain nirvana, one has to love the universe, as opposed to ceasing all feeling.

Meditation results in an accord between you and your experience. It is the slow surge of light towards your soul. Meditation reveals the souls of things within your soul and reveals to you that your soul is immaculately tied to all the other souls in the world; that self and other are but one. One must observe long and calmly for the world to enter into conversation with oneself. In meditation, things coalesce, and space/time is erased. Everything becomes you and you become everything.

Mediation and inspiration go together in the creation of a poem. Sometimes, simply reading a deep and well-crafted line can send the yarn of poetry to unspool and birth a poem that emanates from its truth and beauty. It functions like a nudge, a prick to wake you up to surreal beauty and truth. Poetry sees beauty in everything. It aspires to record it. A poem is never still or frozen in its tracks, but continues its endless tread, entering different hearts through different alleyways. A poem is a living and breathing utterance that has a life of its own with its evolutionary story and despite the poet declaring a poem complete as she concludes its writing, it continues to grow in the hearts and minds of its readers.

Writers and all other artists strive for beauty. They understand that we live for beauty of earthly experience, and to revel in the pleasures of the senses. Without these, survival would have no meaning. When the world is disrupted by tyranny and oppression, its is not just peace and existence that are at stake, but also the beauty of existence that we live for. What is threatened is not just survival, but the very beauty that we stay alive for seems to crumble around us. This is perhaps the reason why ever since times immemorial artists of all kinds have revolted against tyranny. This artistic call springs from their wish to maintain the beauty of the world. They do not just stand up against oppression as a mode of duty, but against the very disruption of the beauty. They stand for the beauty of the universe that springs up in peace, and this encompasses the environment, and other beings.

For writers, the self is inextricably tied to the overt world. Experience for them is always an exchange between the self and the outside world and there is no single place where it begins. It is neither directed inwards nor outwards but is in continual flow. The writing of a poem further closes the distance that one feels from nature and the self and nature become increasingly less estranged with the experience of reading or writing a poem.

This is often explained as a negative capability where the writer becomes nature. However, one can also think that we do not have to negate the sense of self to reach out for the overt. Rather, poetry involves a heightened sense of oneself and an ability to find the universe within the self. One cannot experience that which is not already a part of oneself. Nature is a part of our very biological makeup. A poet has an acute sense of this connection and knows that only that is experienced by us what makes our being. Rilke would not be able to understand the tiger if a part of him, was not already a tiger in a cage. Keats could not have written his "Ode to Autumn," if the seasons did not flutter and flit, already, in his being. They did not negate their subjectivities but meditated long and calm over the presence of these, in their being. The self never disappears in meditating over the universe, but in meditating, one explores and unravels the universe's presence within the self.

By paying attention to an object, one explores not just the object of meditation, but one's own conscious, subconscious, and unconscious to understand it. The resources of understanding the universe are present within one's being. One does not negate subjectivity but explores it to reach an understanding of an overt object. There is no other, but a self with unlimited possibility.

The meditative process in writing leads to revelation. Something of the world is inhaled during the process of meditation and the writer connects this whiff to something in herself. The poet understands that the pursuit of beauty is also that of truth, and that beauty and truth are but one. The poet understands that truth cannot be reached by a scientific dissection of the world that we find ourselves in; rather the truth of existence lies in experiencing the beauty of the universe. The understanding that everything is true, therefore, nothing is true leads one on a cyclical never ending path. Thus, the poet understands that all truth lies in experience.

Suffering that causes innocence to rupture, also leads one to ponder over life. Assessment of the world and life comes about in distress. When assessment of the world is added to its enjoyment the culmination of truth with beauty happens. The impermanence of things leads to pleasure. For the writer this leads to an awakening and openness to experience and an appraisal and enjoyment of beauty while it is still there. Experience gives every poem an essence and ties it up to the essence of the universe itself.

The essence of a poem is deeper than the one intended by the poet, for a poem's essence or soul has a life of its own that is beyond the writer's control. The writer can only create words and not meaning of a poem. The poem has a life of its own, its own existence beyond the lives of the poet or reader. The poet's task is to bring clarity to his own experience and not that of the reader. Poetry is an act of taking flight, and as with every act of flying, poetry too takes one on a journey which must end somewhere with landing back. A poem is a journey through time and space that lifts one up on the wings of imagination and then brings you back on a space where the poem ends but its experience continues beyond the lines. That is the beauty and purpose of a poem—to lead the reader to a mysterious wild place and leave them at its margins to walk around and explore.

The art of concentration in writing, leads the poet to spontaneity. Poetry happens and is not forced into existence. This is not to say that the poet does not think consciously while writing a poem and writes solely from the unconscious pool of feelings and emotions. Poetry is an odd culmination of long-drawn thinking that ends in shaping it with spontaneous overflow. What the poet brings to fruition in a poem, has been pondered over and imagined in the recesses of the mind as well as consciously. Thus, a line in a poem may not be written with much deliberation but for it to come to life, at a particular instant, it must have taken years of culmination. The emotional appeal of a poem comes from the spontaneous, emotional overflow of what has been thought long but is still in the domain of the unknown.

MKB,
August 2021

NATURE

You Do Not Walk Alone

You do not walk alone,
even though a sigh is trapped,
beating against the warm leaf of your heart;
even as the sauntered lake falls into a deserted hollow,
and its sandy bank is barren;
even as the prairies sway without form or friend
and the old barns are sated with memories;
even as the wilted flowers
seem to droop towards eternity's cold gate,
know that you are not alone.
The moving sun across
snowy hills, and the twisted promises of dry trees,
the paw prints walking still, in windswept acres of your heart
and the arms of the wind caressing the clear blue lake
the flowering ripples welcoming a tremor,
and from the moving dawn skies
the birds calling to you,
are home.

Outside, Inside

The universe has fingers
that sift life like stars,
falling, forever falling
like a cliff into us.

Our desires are honey
like the universe's
thick, eyeless darkness

Our hearts are nebulas that
churn red blooded surges of life.
Our blood is suffused with the sun's heat

Our hands always holding on,
are also the gravity of the earth,
holding on to the thin thread of existence

Our eyes are moonshine
that reflect and absorb the
waning and lengthening days

Our pleasures are in returning
our bones to the ash rain,
our flesh to the algae lined hot springs,
our sight to the darkness, and
our breath to the vast wind
that blows through the cosmos
delivering messages to us.

Trees

Your soul hovers in the air, is a latticework of slow sounds.
Sunlight passes through it like a whale song through a lone sea
Your soul crawls deep into the soil
finding a story where the roots roil in mud.
You meditate with every flutter of breath.
Your stillness is a gift.
You stretch to the sky
and the sultry afternoons with love, equally.
Your trunk is now happy and sprightly,
now low, bowing, and heavy,
now still and wan but never ready for death.
Your soul hovers over this morning
and in all your colors,
it knows only one, the color of the sun.
You say something with a sway of stiff arms and
a poet cringes an ear to listen.
A poet pauses like a bird
migrating to another world
and opens her wings on your secrets
to take flight into your still promise,
like dawn entering the night

CLOUDS

Somewhere in the world,
clouds part
like a gift

Elsewhere my spirit flutters in the wind
like a lone flag

Two Seasons

Autumn is a yellow idiom wanting
to burn the flower of
spring in your heart.
It says that it too is a riot,
a celebration, a journey.

Summer calls out.
It is a journey—
fire and light, if you may,
a thread, a leaf,
a butterfly fluttering at your door.

FIRE

From just a seed
a forest will grow.
With just a spark
it will be famished in flames
like old promises lit on expectations

Bird

You do not have to dress in saffron,
or wade through a desert to reach God.
Sometimes your feathers, feet, or fin will suffice.
Have you tried watching a bird wobble or spread its wings
like blossoms opening to the sky, like making it an offering
in its utter restfulness? How much like water she seems,
a forever spilling stream, a gurgle rising from the heart,
and the constantly dripping hive of love in her voice.

You do not have to dress in white,
or wade through a cloud to reach God.
Sometimes the vast sky is Him,
entering the crevices of the world, of you.
Have you tried watching a bird soar into the sky in first flight,
or settle over warm eggs like God's own hand over us
How she is suddenly, the water on the sodden faces of clouds!

You do not have to dress in green,
or wade through a forestto reach God
sometimes the fabric of the forest sings
in his silent voice inside you.
Have you tried to close your eyes and touch
the place inside you, that simply smiles back
at the bird living its many lives in your heart?

THOSE WHO LISTEN

Those who listen to autumn winds
are orange
They do not ask, "what is a tree?"
but simply settle into its easy lair
like autumn's slanting sun pouring
through the lattice of the heart hole
where the love walks in silently

When a listener comes slowly,
a lone tulip blooms on the grave.
It is her prayer,
the culmination of all answers.

EARS

Will anyone listen like the great trees,
that hear winter's breath before it arrives,
invisible as gossamer?
Or like trees that grow towards the heart's sky?
Or like the dawn's golden tongue coaxing the night?

Will anyone listen to the invisible colts
in our hearts
that thump against memory with heavy hoofs
wanting to be birthed again
by the flame flickering in the soul?

Will anyone listen to the breath
we have been holding since
it began with rain and air,
and our breaths—made pure in
the moving fan of the wind
and yet as heavy as the silhouettes of grey clouds?

Between the sky and
the breath's warm promise touching
God's nape, we live through the night.
Will anyone listen to what goes in the dark
in the soul of the universe,
through the night,
through the night?

The Calls of the Forest

The forest calls to me—dark;
the hollow air echoes bird calls
at the inglenook of the heart; the soul warms hands
on its timber; on its buzz, insects float out of
their promise to the anticipating flower

Still and stray, a deer in the heart,
suddenly attentive to the forest, leaps
It is whole and supple and beating
It resumes munching on the ambrosial herbs
as the forest breathes calmly again,
between me and the universe.

THE ELEMENTS

The sky wants you to believe
in the sun rain's juvenile tread
into the tamed animal of your heart,
counting you whole,
devouring your bilateral symmetry,
singling out the heart,
and opening into you one step at a time
First the ten fingers, then the toes,
running your dream water into a river
big enough to fill a rain forest.
Buzzing and sprightly things come
to get a piece of you; you give
and are replenished

The earth wants you to believe
in the cracked soil's breath.
It resurrects your soul
on its dry kiss
and enters you like
the jaguar's roar
filling a jungle.
The pepper vines that
spill their seeds in immersive shock,
and the dandelion's
whiff into the wind,
all balance the soft energy of their bodies
on root and soil.
The earth's truce with air
teaches you stillness

But before you arrive at stillness,
your body must expand
like a puffed pigeon
coming out of its wings

in a fading flutter,
and stretch taut over the face of the drum
that is your soul.

The elements touch all the chambers
of winter inside you.
They nudge you to take flight
and see
that the road to nowhere
begins here: at the hem of music

The Mango Tree

The tree is lost in its leaves
like the day is lost every passing hour melting into dusk.
Its branches stretch, over which
green beads herald mangoes.
Every day it plunges for salubrious ambrosia
Into the Earth's raw heart
But despite all the mud draughts
it fruits only every other year.
As we were here, looking at trees,
crouching under snowy stalks,
trees that had shed old promises,
the lone mango stood behind us,
its whiff already at our napes,
its arms burdened and unburdened many times,
its dark soul heaved with secrets that
we can no longer know,
because we did not see it growing.
Now, we cannot put our ears to it
to partake in its vibrant song
or to unfold its secretive soul, once more;
so proud are we of our promises to
this new land
where snow clouds the insides of life
in shiver and fret

When the Seasons Speak

Through the many lives of seasons
we see insects come and go,
flowers grow and wilt,
the night stretched taut on the drum of fears, sometimes,
sometimes moonlight and beauty.
The mornings are mostly bright,
and the noons pant their way to night,
or are dull and slowly lumber up the day's steep cliff.
We see the seasons passing through our lives,
but the universe sees through
the briefest moment of our hearts

When the Pandemic is Past

Inside, it is starry
like a galaxy,
outside, the rain pours on.

The swivel of light at every bend,
as panting and breathless it descends,
into the heart made sore,
is sad, but true.
We have learnt to live
in the rocky encampments of the heart
and to say prayers in stony voices over the graves
of the dead.

When all this is over
we will hold each other's palms
to feel life awakening
dizzily like a great bear
coming out of hibernation,

and outside, it will no longer rain.
But some stars in the heart will have lost their light

JOURNEYS INTO THE WORLD

You can trace in air
the journey of birds
through the cloudy forehead of God
revealing only this much
to itself, to you.
Life does not come out of the box of place
You need not unwrap it like a gift
It is the root mesh
that flourishes
synapse-like
between you and the world falling
about you like a floppy sunhat
And one by one the
butterfly flutter
leaves your chest
and you find yourself
full of their absence,
never empty.

Being Deaf in Music

When the music leaves the sky
with swirling seagulls,
it is wet in the sunset. Before the sky turns onyx,
and leaves the bare branches
of the tree to inhale peace,
the first wind dances slowly.
In slow wait of light, the houses
on the heaving breast of the mountain
turn on lights that howl lonely like a wolf.
There is no clank of noise here,
only the wind rustling husky in the leaves
My eyes are dreamy from the first sip of fullness,
my lips taste motherhood in the milk of the moment.
Freedom rings with every sound the sky resonates.
I see signs. I cringe my eyes to understand the language
of nature floating in the earth's womb
like old stories shivering in the dark

What Can We Give the Earth?

It gives us these rains slashing through the wind of our dreams;
the lone dear crossing the margin of supple imagination;
the marigolds of searing in the monsoon rain;
the flowers' cup of love, and the root suckling the milk earth;
the soft scent of sunspots;
the hand of love petting our savannah souls,
and the singular pact between the soul and the universe—
the soul spread like a quilt covering the universe.

What can we give to the curve of the earth's promise,
that sits like an egg between our folded hands?
The slow surge of tides rises between us and the earth.
What can we give, empty as we are?
And the scent we think rises from our bodies, rises from
the earth's many secretive lives.

LOVE

LOVE'S GREAT STORY

I am love's great story,
a heart beating inside an old oak tree,
and a voice like the chords of sunlight.
I wonder how I got here, between
the forest, and the frozen lake by the body's heavy mound.
I walk the lengths of moonbeams
to arrive at your soul

I am love's great story,
but I am also a wandering bark
on a foggy lake, looking through the haze
for the golden moon of your face.
I feel your pulse where my throat meets
the ears of a twinkling lake,
I hear every word before it is said
and feel the touch of every risen ripple.
I step into the cool water of your deep sighs.
I worry that the damp room of your soul is spent.
I cry when peacocks spread wings in a lone dance,
and cry when drizzling the rain halts.

I am love's great story
I try to walk through the drums of war beating on my heart,
and understand that every feeling is the feeling of love:
no sorrow, no envy, no worry, but a bird
that takes flight from love's empty window
I am made of only stiff words that vanish traceless.
I breathe the only language there is.
I dream where the soul sways into the cosmos.
I try and try but cannot arrive at the one answer.
But still, I hope
because I am love's great story

Ten Love Poems for Amrit

I

Window

How I wish the stars would twinkle a little more today
and sing a lullaby to put the tired eyes to sleep.
I leave the window open for the love to
come in soft whiffs through it.
A tune is always rolling in my heart, that is also yours.
It is like laughter that rolls on happy morns and like the sun
rolls through the sky into the folds of the evening,
and into the depths of the rising soul—
my soul rising into yours

II

Where Souls Intersect

there is neither light, nor darkness,
no foreboding sorrow spilling on our path,
nothing to trace where we've been,
only the slow feeling of love spinning
in its clear happiness.

It is bliss that sprouts every spring
like buds manifesting from the earth's folds,
a steady flow of thick nectar—
love is a candle
that burns through lightyears. Its whiff is in the dreamy heart,
and its light courses the hollow spaces in the spirit.

III

You are a Tree

You are a redwood stroking
the mauve cloud of my imagination.
Your arms are nests
where the bird of my heart hides.
The quiver of breeze in your boughs,
is an opera of birth
The wind in your green dreams
is my breath seeking out an echo.
It has been spinning since the orbs started reeling.
When the sky behind your form
is a riot of clouds going every-which-way
and your scent beckons me,
I walk straight into your flutter and fire.
My ear to your heart,
I hear the sky's slow wail rising
up from the sodden grass at your feet.
When the buds of my desire sprout
through yours, they bend my head
in humble obeisance to
the prayer in your heart.
The blossoms are slivers of our story,
each bud encasing a memory,
each bee hovering over them, seeking
a passage into eternity,
and each rain drop collecting in the cup of petals
is a sip of divine ambrosia.
The scent of life rising from your boughs
hovers between the sky and its sounds, and
runs through my veins like golden blood
gilding my waning soul

IV

You Open a Door in Me

You are the summer passing through my
narrow autumn like falling stars singing
through the night sky.
Your heart is a gift to the world, and here
is poised in love's perennial garden.
The hot sky fills the universe with your blaze.
You fill me with all the colours, and with the
heart of winds that flutter at the altar of my desire.
You are the first golden daffodil
that blooms on the thin crust of hope and
your whiff of faith settles in me
like water settles in a lake

The frogs that croak in rainy puddles are never silent.
When it pours, she calls her lover.
Her croaks are the language of love.
His call back is an avowal of beauty
that enters through the doors of the music.

V

When the stray cat that came by
in yesterday's wounds, is walking in circles;
and a creeper scampering up a tree
is vain in its pursuit of heights;
when the hot wind from the ocean
beholds only a mirage,
I know our entwined hands will one day
be unclasped.

Remember then, that I remain.
I'll leave footprints—
like a wolf passing through the sparkling snow.
Know then, that the swirling wind
will unload its cloud
and I will be there
in the glinting deposit of sand.
Remember the trees and you will be home.
Know then, that you will find me
wherever raw scent will silently roam.
When long drawn days fall into spite,
know that you will find me in every waning night.
Look up at frayed flakes of ash as they
dance down the sky.
Know that you'll find me in rooted fire, and
in its sparks and ash that fly.
In the heat and the green, in blood and spleen;
I will trickle down with the rain,
I will be in every sodden grain.
You will find me all around
because here and now are
the same as there and then
You will hear me in fall and rain.
You will feel me in the sun and snow.
And kiss me on the flowers' open mouths.
Yet I remain,

Yet I dance,
Yet the swiveling of soul with soul
sounds out a song

VI

Blindness

Tonight, you open the soles of my feet
and rise in the capillary tubes of my bones,
the grains of years drawn on them.
Every circle is an avowal of your heart.
You keep rising to the desert of the soul
Blind and silken, the winds
filter past the windows of the irises.
Slow stones turn on their backs
at the tremors of your arrival.
Memory flows, thirsty for whiffs of your starry night.
The heart's four chambers are dry
until you drizzle your fire in a slow rain of sparks..
Then, as you lock your eyes into mine,
thunder flies the birds of love
to their nest is in my soul
and we go blind in the never-ending rain of love.

VII

I Leave You This

The tang of an autumn rose wedded
to the thorn hand of summer.
This vastness of the promises of the sun,
the ash that remains after fire,
the nebula of desire.

I welcome you to wade through this river
Water adorns your feet as it fills up
between the toes like silver rings.
This caress of water is supple and with
an understandable Creole in its mouth.

I leave you the crumpled sheet of the sky
with layers of rain
rising forever from a forgotten salt sea towards me,
but also reveling in slow wait to float the wind
through the fields of desire with their warm moist hands

I leave you the first page of this book
Before contents or acknowledgement
This vast blankness of wait.
This one that keeps its scent intact.
A beginning that asks and ventures,
That is unclothed and not yet stone

I leave you the moss
on the hill face of my desire
soaking down your rain.
It furrows and fissures through stem and rock,
like a meteor cuts through the sky's many constellations.

I loosen my fist
to let the years slip through
and descend like threads of music.
You jump, you reach out to it like

a sunflower reaches out to the sky.
My promise waves in the wind, in the sky
up above in the clouds, and in
an empty space where sight refuses to see.
The air moves like a song

VIII

Waiting for the Festival of Lights

When the sun sags into the damp puddle
at the feet of dusk that walks into our lives,
the wind in unison with the sun sings a last song.
It echoes through a misty mountain,
its head in a reverie, and
slides into the foggy breaths that make up the soul.
Just as sunset ruptures the day,
I wait for you to emerge round
and windy from a dandelion stub
into the heart of the red rose of my passion.
Something of you was deposited already
in the salt of my noontides.
My tongue, it betrays
the taste of a syrupy moon
to taste your salinity.
My desire waits to rise with your tidal eyes.

I am a stone baked in your reverie
I am a thousand lamps
at the altar of your dream
I am the wick, and oil,
the wind that beats the heart of fire.
I am the festive prayer, the color of celebration,
the incense of a jasmine bush.
I know you will follow my scent back
and come in the season of light

IX

In Your World

Sometimes when I'm in another season,
monsoon rivulets suddenly spread where
your eyes have wandered on my soul.
They dissolve it into the lachrymose of a true rain

The slow whirlwinds of your arms
drain me of dimension and
open an eye in my abdomen.
The tune in your heart is a prophesy.

My garden is already ripening with the wisdom of love.
Our single back grows
like the age-old neem by the lake of fire.
It is soaked into the sun of desire.

You plant a garden of roses.
You see where the petals grow from the stem of my heart.
You melt the lightening into light, and
and squeeze out silver linings from the clouds
to nurture the spaces within us.

X

Dreams Continue into Reality

1.

A dream of doves, their feet tied together
does not fall into an abyss when reality comes.
When the silken curtain rises on our love,
the smoke of prayer rises heaven-ward
and from just a tear, the rest of the body forms.

2.

When our marriage consummates,
something begins to till reality
out of the pits of a thousand flutes.
The length of dreams must have corners
that are folded by a childhood whim.
In a single night I am alive

3.

Life leaves a rose bud and enters the
many open mouths of my ocean,
like the very first batch of fish
entering the robes of the water.

4.

I look
and a sunspot, seawater, a cross-stitch,
a dust of pollens, a pod of cotton
tapping, engraving, stimulating.
In this robe, something rubs my feet,
and awakens me from my fainting fit.
In this robe, I am everything

Unearthing

I

(Outdoors)

For Fatch

That wind was butter
on a stony sky.
Frisky fingers unpack a gift
of dry leaves, red at the margins.
Where they fumble is a secret
wrapped in the velvet of weeds.
I look again to where a mound
is cracking its once soapy skin
(clay become a crumble).
And now spring roots pucker at its powder.
Underneath is a cave,
(not an archeologist's discovery
but the mint sap and cane juice
of my childhood).
It is baked and orange now
like a vase of disheveled
rusty sunflowers.
This secret that has stayed
but stopped singing in a chorus in the head,
that no longer arranges its body
like a wasp alighting on a flower
but fades and famishes
and gives you this cave from my hands
I built it with you,
the summer sun baked it,
and time covered it with soil.
Now the garden gives it back,
our cave growling no more,

quietly, the garden growing shoots into its stone,
our cave, famished and lonely

II

(Indoors)

For my grandmother

The stiff air is opaque
and I bump into things
rotten from the last monsoon
It has left it tracks—the silence of its
salty, sandy trail of a small rivulet
I follow it though I have not forgotten
the way to the storeroom,

where no longer can I find
the tin box of biscuits with
pale green buttons, pencil stubs,
smooth cotton handkerchiefs,
and my grandmother's collyrium.
I fumble at the light
It goes on like
the last hum in a building,
when the workers leave the evening to it.
The white porcelain
is gone,
scattered among us
who survive still.
The smell here is brown tattered, almost surgical.
This room inhales clouds of scent,
the life metaphor sucked out of it.
The roof is brick, the windows are wood
but it is not iron that holds it together.
It is this ligament and tissue
of our shuddering souls,
the cartilage that listens,

the morning film over eyes
that want to see past the fog of opaque air,
the synapse that allows the message to skip,
the wound growing collagen,
the simple white of her eyes—
still, silent and long,
preserving the tears—
subsurface and clear.
The misty sight we remember
from her spectacles—
we tend to it now with only memory
and we always feel there is no post life
but still wish for a place,
post summer
post window and curtain
post the ordered shelf
of mirror, brush, and eye drops
post, post, till we can see
to feel your nearness still.

The Flood

for my brother, Fatch

Years ago, when the weather alighted on us,
we looked for places to hide,
nestled under banana leaves,
splashed under grape boughs until the flood
poured over us its dim shadow.
How could it rain that much?
How could water, that was so thin,
drown entire cities?
A part of us did not believe them.
A part was silently terrified.
Monsoons later, I still wonder,
what color sky was it that had shed such agony?
What immersed these promises in pain?
When my grandmother talks of how rain
is good for the paddy crop, I wonder
if she has seen that flood; but I see
her glassy eyes have seen more,
much more.
But is seeing ever enough,
is seeking?

INNOCENCE

For Papa

When father varnishes the bench in our lawn,
strange birds give him company.
Their cacophony is mild as they look   quietly, searching, searching,
pecking at minuteness spread   as seeds, and
fidgeting with dry leaves.   What discoveries do they yearn?
Then slowly as they had collected, they dissipate and
the air has stiff starched holes of their absence.

Tomorrow, father will weed the garden.
The weeds will acquiesce with bowed heads,
and the worms will slither out in the root-space,   roiling in the weeds'
slushy soul,
reminding us how death creeps into life   slow but determined.

Years ago, he said, "believe,"
on that rickety evening when I almost let go
of the ships sailing in my head.
I worried myself stiff thinking about
the dimming star in my soul stream—
this fire running through the veins that had stopped cackling.
Under the blood is the garden where my dog is buried.
In between him and me   is an icy cave running rivers of fire.

When father shows a rose   that bloomed quietly in the night
I imagine the dark weaving into it   its scent.
Even as he pointed to it, his quietness filled up the garden
and tumbled in hope. He is like a newborn foal learning to walk.
(I am learning too from what remains,
learning to listen between the silences, and
relearning sentence structure.)
Some years ago I had his gait; before Bollywood undid mine.
One can see the jolts in his easeful walk,

how the shoulders stutter but the feet sway smoothly.
What he conceals is betrayed.
But when he is mending his lawn, his back to the sun,
innocence settles around him like birds alighting onto the ground.
These wings cast a shade over us
and sometimes we too begin to decipher the message
this bird brings   quietly, unabashedly, to this place—
to the dim, dark caves gnawed into us—from an abyss away.
Its birdsong is stiff as a blizzard buried in its snow,
but some winds rustle   in the worn willows of our hearts
telling us there are still mornings   lined up against every desert,
where the oases patiently await unseen in their spring.

Sometimes His Silence Speaks

For my green-cheeked conure, whom I call Koko

He never shrieks when you are near
He takes a bath in the spilling song of a shower
that never holds him in its supple embrace
like the wind never holds the rain and
the rain never holds the tree
He is light, yet the heaviness of a promise
settles around when he circles the air above our heads.
He asks us many times, about home
like a leaf inquiring the rain about its tireless journey from the ocean

I don't know his smile
and yet I try to decipher if he is happy or sad
I have seen the colors that pour
out of him like a tall waterfall;
Sometimes they are in his wide-open eyes,
sometimes the way he wobbles or flits,
and the way he calls when you are near.

DEVOTION

for Koko, my green-cheeked conure

She perches herself onto my shoulder and speaks
It is sometimes a question, sometimes a demand,
and sometimes, just a call—a singular twitter
that sheds confused sentences into the mind.
How well can you know a bird, it's whale promise
rising from a heart smaller than a beat, but housing
entire chambers of the Pacific? Can you swim
like a fish down to its deepest trenches? Can you taste
every plankton and catch every sunbeam?
From the fronds of her heart, can you pluck a meadow?
Or less likely, can you hold the darkness of
empty rooms between you and her?
How far can you go
into the profound promise she makes to you
or into her devotion to you? Her pause at your voice,
and the flutter of a yawn mean many things.
Her devotion to you is ever ripe, like a tree.
It grows roots into you and cracks the walls you make
around your soul. She teaches your numbness to flower.
She sends your faith rocketing to the sky.
Green as the savannah in spring,
she leads your soul like the wind leads the rain. Every rustle
of trees that touches your soul, is her place of devotion.

In a Winter Land

For my green cheeked conure, Koko

You will only see her if she is nestled in the snow.
There, she is a green spot
on February's splurge of white.
She was born in the colourful saturations of summer,
in the wild trims of its canopy-growth.
The forest is her invisible dress.
She knows not the touch of dry brittle icicles,
but has savoured all the floods of the Amazon.
The sky's mind flows through her
and simply, miraculously, she reads it,
like I never will.
The juice-red hook of her beak
is sure of the saccharine taste of berries.
The floating promise of a splash
in the tropical rain is enough to
send her into an unspooling flutter.
But she has learnt to live in winter's inverted shadow.
In winter she becomes visible,
her black eyes like black stars
in a white sparkling sky that sheds
strange songs of snow and desire.

Love Resides in These, Too

Gossamer- the finest thread; sometimes,
the first discovery of the day,
the holder of water and life,
the spider's gift to the garden,
the summer's thin belief, floating
freely between the silent love
of the morning and things.
You will breathe it in, odorless
and it will stick to your form, invisible.
It will be there every morning waiting for you

Inglenook- the earth's place in the Solar System,
the perfect distance between things that sense
and things that incite,
an old man's comfort, a fireman's despair.
We live a dream of inglenooks
yet we know that
fire will be the final abode of the soul

Penumbra- the cast-off lightness of things,
the body splitting in a joyous dance into
the many arms and hands of a goddess, and
the hidden meanings of life trying to take shape.
It is always there waiting in luminous halos
to engulf the whole shadow in its pastel glows

Petrichor- the smell of earth after rain,
a taker to the unremembered and hidden.
It is minuteness hovering,
heralding the love that imbues the
water with the soil. Energy flows
out of the elements, and enters us,
the smell changes into color.
We see that we are green, and slowly ripening

45

Lagoon- a rare island of water.
You can imagine it even if you've never seen it.
It reflects like all water, it wears robes of ripples,
cajoles us into living, then makes
us fall, only to find that it is not alone,
that we are not alone

THOUGHTS,
in POETRY

IMMORTALITY

None will survive:
not the ivy scampering up the tree,
not the winged fury of an eagle,
not the surprised squirrel,
not the sun, now blinding the noon sky,
not the fresh bubbles of a spring stream,
not the rainbow voices of mockingbirds,
not the rayon touch of a dog's fur,
not the sky's lash of monsoon rain,
not the buckled man's searing pain,
not the man hunting on his hill,
not the woman sewing torn stockings,
not the windy geese crossing the ocean,
not the sudden deer on the road,
not the golden fleece of sheep at sunset,
not the beckoning promises of lovers,
not the dry road of old age,
not the fresh butter floating in a water dish
not the man reciting verses in a temple,
not the war sanding our hearts with stone

Our fears pass through life's prism
and scatter every which way.
We are wounds hiding in lairs,
but do we pass through this rain
without a word or nod?
Listen, it has been delivering
hope in its silent tongue.
Never the hope of immortality,
but a silent hope of wakefulness.
Can we learn the language and read
the dawn's writing to dusk?
All because we will not survive

Guru Nanak into the Light[1]

The river cutting through fog
calls him and he must go.
On the way,
the trees with fronds for hearts,
the flowers with balmy hands
of petal and pollen,
the honeybees
spun on wings and nectar,
and the lone grasshopper
landing on the mind's jasmine hand,

are us too.
Their lives happen
also in the body's brief spark, and
the head's deep halo of nectar.
The breathing brittle light spewing
from dawn's splintering clouds
violet from the bruise of mornings,
are us too.

From the moment Nanak entered
into the river until three days later
when he emerged out of it
is a void in the stretch of the universe,
a soundless unstirring place

Did Nanak feel the
crunch of grass underfoot
or the drowsy sandy bank

1. Guru Nanak Dev is the first guru of the Sikhs. There goes a story from Guru
Nanak's life that one winter night as he was meditating by a river, he got up and walked
into the river. People looked for him without any success. It seemed as if he had vanished
without a trace. Three days later, he emerged from the river and said the words that make
up the *Japuji Sahib*, a holy text of the Sikhs. This incident is symbolic of Guru Nanak's
enlightenment.

that squished like marigolds
in the syrup of his tread?
Before the night poured
him through its ancient eye
could he hear the universe's
virile growl of "Om"?
When he walked into
the water's plush bed,
was he welcomed with
the oceanic smell of life?

The villagers only
saw him come out
and when he emerged,
he said,
"There is only one God.
Truth is His name."

Every day, as morning prayer fills the room,
I imagine God, a universal musician
scattering and gathering us,
and we are all tunes
wandering and wanting to
unite our fragmented notes
with the universe's "Om."
Each of us is a light
rising up the morning sky
looking and listening for
what is already buried
at the horizons of the mind, that
calls from night's eyeless seed.
And we must go.

THE HEART'S ONLY WISH

The heart wants a little fire.
It does not want a reason to live.
Through the confusing cast of a penumbra,
it welcomes light,
but it does not want a reason to live.
It knows how to do that too well.
It has practiced living since before birth.
The heart is sure that it will fly
even though the wounded wings
seem heavy in the touch of wind.
And yet, it wants to tread old paths
like a record spinning a wobbly tune
over and over as it is circled by music.
It wants to burn in the fire in the distance
that has lit up a lone tree in the kitchen window,
as if embracing it
and saying, "You are not alone. We are not alone."

Memory

Is memory a great epic, told in a darkening evening,
an event that inhales the last breath many times,
an edifice, or moving pictures in the mind?
Sometimes, it feels like a coral reef
growing forever with life,
a skeleton mound, a dump of skulls
by the lake of life, that collects before
it gives up everything like a woman shedding
the starry cloak of night from her body, that is a river.

Maybe it is a ball of yarn you can
knit into quilts, crocheted and
donning holes for the passage
of voice, and image
through it.

Or is it like a vacant field,
the size of the cosmos, where the body meets
the last cry of life in a star or a stone,
a depositor of dreams—gay,
an annexe of desires—rotten,
and the old storyteller
wearing a coat for days when the rain never stops?

It is as old as life itself,
it leans on you, the dog, and the grasshopper,
it came before you were born,
and before the grasshopper landed on your ear,
and the dog in your heart.
Maybe, the memory of fire and mountains,
was there before the universe
started winding its ancient clock

BLOOD, MILK, AND NECTAR

Inspired by Frida Kahlo's 1940 painting,
"Self Portrait with Thorns and Hummingbird"

Butterflies in her braided locks
hum mating songs.
Birth is nestled in-between
their fluttering and her mind which is,
folded memories.
The body's splurge into
hollow darkness,
where translucent butterflies fantasize
dreams of birthing fires,
where being is a fountain, a star, a song
and the soul waits to be led to its lair
through a forest of painted last leaves.

Sounds surge up in the
apertures of this painting,
as slowly a forest blooms from colour
into bird song and nectar.
The blood knows her story—
the one she delicately arranges in
a vase of pain.
She forges fruits in her blood—unborn babies.
She feed them with her life milk,
and spools them in nectarine threads
like making a large cocoon for the
butterfly of her heart.

A necklace of thorns chokes.
She is crucified at the altars of a mishap
like we all are.
This necklace, she wears as a cross,
it drips blood into an abyss

that never echoes back,
and her heart falls forever into the dark.
The hummingbird at its hem

flutters.

It is mothered too.
mothered but also with memory of a lair
where it is headed.
Her life falls about her soul like a body.

Is she a fountain or a friend?
Is she petted by the universe's certain hand?

Peering from the darkness—a cat,
and rapt in itself—a monkey,
are two lives tied to hers,
immaculately close, expressly loving
But there is nothing—she feels— nothing
like the embrace between
mother and child, a brew of
blood, milk, and nectar.

Cast Off

I cast off myself like a salaam,
like the schism of the unknown
This gesture of pouring forth language
is deference to the flower
that sprouts lonely by night
and by day, opens into a garden.

I cast off myself, like a woman dismisses a thimble
after the noisome giddiness of
Embroidering still life—
a basket of plucked flowers,
that will be next week,
the burning brambles for the night.

I dismiss the mysteries of the dark
to dream like a bear in spring
wading through life that rises anew
through the breaths of changing seasons.

Like a sky shedding dying birds,
I shed myself like this: the dark night's
azure hand, falling evermore in others'
placid lives, dazing the ataxia of my flames
and placing my soul
like a vase in love's window.

Hibernation

I sleep
in autumn's fiery fingers.
I freeze
soon after the first dead fog
has lit the winter on my pyre.
It drenches me with its freezing thirst for stillness.

I arrive at life only after
my blood has frozen
in the sieves of the heart
and no longer pours forth
but every beat remembers its warmth
and every day I light a candle
at the altar of the vulnerability
of the hibernating animal of my soul.

WINTER

I don't regret the winter, only the breathless world
in whose mouth it comes like fog.
I don't regret the winter, only its cold face that whips
my blood till it becomes rubies in the dead flower
of my exhaustion.
I don't regret the winter, only it rusts me
on the inside and blows away
like the whiff of wind on a dandelion
I don't regret seasons that
leap into a love for lost things

A Finding

A moth, the color of wood,
fluttered on the zoologist's window while he slept.
Some time at night, it fell on the dusty pane
and spread its wings for the last time.
When the biologist wakes up the next morning
he had-his-tea-went-on-a-walk.
All this while the moth lay in its eternal rest.
Then by-chance as he was looking for a book,
he saw a part of a yellow, and
the yellow extended to orange,
then became brown, then black.
He looked and the wings grew into
an abdomen, into a head of eyes.
He picked it up and placed it on the dissection table.
It stopped growing.
Living demands collecting water drops,
is a trembling pebble under every step.
      How odd, in a world of eyes a
      moth can live unseen for years.
      How odd, in a world of borders
      a moth crosses the jungle and comes to this window.
How odd, he names the moth after himself

A Normal Photo

In this photo are two people, subtracted
for a time from all those others.
For once, I am conscious of the margins.
The photo has a world beyond
its five sides, and there is one side
they are looking out at where something
always hovers beyond the horizon.

As we look at this photo,
what is happening to the tree behind us?
Will it still be standing here next time we come?
Has a bird started making a nest in its branches?
From the thousand leaves,
which leaves will shed today?
Will someone observe under their feet,
the distance from dry leaf to dust?
Someone unknown to me must have
swept clean the premises in the morning fog
and someone will come by the evening
to shake this very earth into a kaleidoscope.

Last Time

The last brush stroke in a painting
emerges yellow from red and
green reclines in the margins.
The last drop shivers on a thawing
tree. Half of it falls in the puddle,and
the other half, lonely, dries
Every day has a last time
when the room is left, locked
with curtains drawn to the sun.
No one knows the last time of
a rainbow in the sky.
How long can one watch?
Last times are the norm.
Sometimes the last time is fog or wind,
sometimes an avowal of new life.
There is the last fruit in the kitchen garden
drying seeds for next spring.

The Mercy of Birth

*For those to whom the birth of a child is redemptive,
and those who cannot hear*

She was deaf
and when the cherry blossoms turned black
she whistled out of them songs of agony.
Scuttling in her throat, words fell
like the heat drapes of the sun, and
blunt poison craters led her mouth to their brims.
She prayed with palms pressed to the cranky
clouds that would not take her to the sky,
'til a little mercy awoke in her night
of frothy stars.
She held this little hand and counted
little hopes on her palms.
She sang a hymn of respite
in her throat of thorns
'til the dawn spread its still antlers.
It was a flute floating out of the woods;
dimpled mercy that was
too small to hold, too big to let go.

Epitaph

Here rests a line drawn on the map of the world
that runs through latitudes,
joins places with the same time but different time zones;
when the wind crosses her, its name changes.
No one drew her on the earth,
and no one plucked her away.
Now she is finally established as
a longitude in her grave and reads 180 degrees.
The date changes here.
And she will no longer turn
because the earth is finally not flat.

This Might be What Poetry is Made of

I

How a single sentence tosses a whiff of the cosmos!
The mind leaps into the universe's outer shadow,
into the evening's receding tar,
that is also the colour of space.
The night inside is crystal in its resonant knell
the cougars by the waning pond of life
inspire a sentence
and out pours a violet evening
from the heart's luminous eye.
Uncurling its river
it streams and straightens
between the lush boughs of desire.

I try to saunter away out of spring's last sleep in my mind,
the hibernating poems already stirring, and
the provenance of verses—a window of birth.
My poems are essays into the subtle scent of life.
The clouds in my mind make me a magician.
This canoe lost somewhere in Lethe; it tides up my sleeve
into the crimson sun of my throat.
Like Shiva's throat, like a fingerprint, it is translucent and
houses always the blue light of a poisonous sky,
except, this poison is wispy dark/blind.
It spreads and covers me
'till the sentences are music
and a poem has spawned
from the deep echoes of empathy.

II

The creaky garden of a poem opens its grounds.
It comes folded between leaf and shoot.
There is a vacancy where its marigold eyes
look into mine.
The irises by the reflective pond are dead no more.
This withering curtain of the wind
blows old tunes into the faces of clouds.
The shattered mirrors of the pond
hold my geranium image,
each flower a moment, each poem an eternity.
And when a poem has been written,
birds fly from my arms to the sky,
and I see a moving landscape
from the steady gallop of train's window.
I leave the birds for your eyes.

III

My poems burn and wane
like the shadows of the moon in a pouring halo of dreams.
Their flambeau spreads like the somnolent sky
And spins dreams into a dull life.

The poem drums on the sky and squalls of crows
appear at its vacant face.
I catch them in my poems. I catch
their weight and onyx to pen a blood crop.
It lightens the sultriness of my fever.
It is an arctic dream born in black torridity,
a wharf at the end of the ship.
I write and wait, wither and make
'till the vacant is filled by the barren.
When the poem has been penned,
vacancy settles where my poem was
Something cumbersome straightens in my mind
I rest.

IV

Sometimes starry skies speak
my language: it is rain.
Swans in puddles of my desire float,
the smoke rises, and
rises farther up
'till it fills up the throat's nectarine funnel with
the gurgling spring of a poem—
this shooting geyser,
this locked word that keeps knocking,
knocking its heavy sky fist on my heart.
It fissures and floats on the boiling magma of love,
It buries forests in its desert mouth
for you to see its beauty.
It is the beauty of a wind-beaten tree,
of stars slowly shaping the night, and
of a lone splash in the distance
that stills everything.

V

A door is shut behind my eyes
the creepy hand still on the knob
All this while fresh smoke rises through the
split space between the door and the frame.
Slowly, a footstep appears
imprinting the wet sand by the lake of the heart.
Birds flap open in my hands,
and the poem is only
a flight of blood to the numb corners
in my throat. A butterfly touches its syrup belly
to the stem of life.
The wind is still beneath my skin,
rolling, rolling in the slush of the soul.

VI

I have heard poems
rippling on rocks.
They are rapids
I have held poems that are spirits of the ocean, and
that float boats cutting through whale song.
Poems are fresh pearls and floating fireflies
pass through their fingers
I have witnessed the sunrise of a poem
between mountain and vale.
Little wildflowers hold open
cupped hands catching the first
milk of daybreak; just being born,
the poet sips what drips from the rolling cup of a river
as life sounds in the jungle's green echo.

THE POOR MAN WHO GAVE BASKET RIDES

There are times the mountains move.
At night they shift their weight on sappy feet
                    and dance.
That man who lumbered up them,
carrying strangers' children in a basket on his back,
knew this well, all too well. He'd seen the creases of
ridge and cliff rise and fall in the horizon of his window
like the mountains were lumbering, panting.
Every night as he lay his stiff shoulders on the day's last breath
the mountains moved farther
and his little shack leaning on the valley let out a sigh
like a pet animal waiting to be fed.
Dreams were rare. Nights were rich.
And sometimes, if it had been a kind day,
unbeknownst to himself, he smiled in his sleep.
The stranger who had, that day,
innocently shared with him her food,
smiled too in hers, farther away, but in a leaning cabin too.
And under the supple sky, the mountains
held hands and sang a little rhyme,
a lullaby to rock them as they slept
silently through their nights.

I Write to You, Home

I write to you, home,
to the wild caress of your weed heart
that calls me to return every spring to your garden.
I always return to you, no matter how
intimidating the destinations of my travel have been—
their surf sultry, their limbs rowing gondolas,
their language lapping like hungry animals in my mouth,
their paws printed on my heart's story, like old wounds.
Between my nails, their soil has deposited moon tales
or the flushed happiness of a brakeless run, down a mountain—
I will always return home because
it says: I have been here for you, waiting.

KASHMIR

When spring comes to dawn
flowers will grow from
the tired hearts of trees,
spreading over their old souls like a shroud,
swimming in their breaths,
after every winter of waiting.
In the breath of the north wind
flowers sigh in bare trees.
Flowers sigh dead in the soil.
Kesar blossoms rot splattered in blood.
Spring waits and war rages.
Flowers will not bloom on this side of Kashmir,
on the Kashmir, as cold and beautiful
as a glass rose that bloomed, but is now frozen in time.

We Want to Hide

from the hot wind searing our flesh,
from the chill and sting of an Arctic spite,
from the love kiss waiting
under the lush hand of your desire,
from the sun and its sweltering promises,
from the moon mixing
old dreams into your nights,
from the beetle climbing
up the wall of wisdom towards you, and
from the topple you can take
on the tight rope of dreams.

It is not late yet, to gather
the summer wind and Arctic chill, and
to welcome home the sun and the moon.
Here, is the world where there is
nothing before, or behind, or betwixt.
This here, settles in us,
like a bird's warm belly settling on eggs.
Meanwhile, soundless and stirring,
the aurora borealis dances for our attention.

The Universe Puts on an Attire

The universe puts on an attire,
pulling its hair in a knot
of clouds and dust,
sweltering ribbons of
stars yet to be born, whirl;

an attire of light
and the cosmos—naked—shines
through its sheer fabric
like the many prayers
on the translucent wall of dreams;

an attire of glorious morns—
With sunny promises to the trees and us
and to the enlivened
pulse under the galloping colts
of desire;

an attire of trees
green with the soft spin
of life in them, drying and dying
into the macrocosm's vast hand,
but splattering seeds of love, still;

an attire of you and me,
our faint but steady heartbeats
in the growing drone
of the spinning orbs
are a knock on its door and
it allows life to enter,
It is
never unclothed, never bare, because
the universe puts on an attire
to paint doors at the awakenings of our souls.

Every Day I Tell Myself this Story

Be not surprised at change
for when the spring retracts
its snuggle of blossoms and wilts
at your doorstep, it nudges you to float out
of your flower bed for a draught of true passion.
Know then, that you are not
a soul in the dark.

Be not surprised at sorrow
for when the winter mewls
and cries its stormy promise
with a cloud around your head,
and you wander deep into your soul,
Know then that there is
delight in wandering inward,
near.

Be not surprised at your frailty,
at the smooth edges of your desire,
at your fingers that reach
out to other hands but always
have iron fists guiding your heart.
Know then that at the altar of the soul
your vulnerability will suffice.

Be not surprised that innocence
will wander away. Think of the
sparrows of childhood that have
another home now, closer to the Arctic,
closer to the sea, on its other side.
Know that when you look over the sea to
find a lost home, you are your home too.

Know that it started lightyears ago

with sound announcing the cosmos.
We are all sounds, fragmented notes.
Know that all the tunes you have inhabited
are floating towards life, towards you.
You are a ballerina in nature's grip.
It handles you, and dips you, and
swivels you around its arm, it returns
your embrace with the universe
as you open arms to its nebulous lightness.

THE DELUGE

When it rains
in silken threads all year long;
rains and washes away the ashen faces of tyranny;
rains and washes away the bruises on benches
where once someone deposited their sorrow for the world,
and bruises the size of hearts;
rains and washes away the blood dripping soils across
the steppes, and prairies,
the pampas and downs;
rains and rises with blood running up the trunks of
acacias and mangroves, palms, and oaks, and
all the flowers so still, as if they were dead,
I think of all the rebels and their enemies,
and how we can all be washed away
by a tsunami the size of hatred.
The weight of oceans
can drown down the wails of the world
without a trace. In a million years more,
we will be lost fossils and there will
be no stories to tell of all
that happened before the flood:
all the wars
and colonization, and bloodshed.
All for nothing
All ending in nothing

Nirvana

We wish to go there, where
nothing is:
no hot nor cold, damp nor dry,
frayed nor starched, near nor far,
loath nor love, wild nor tame;
where nothing is sown into the soul's tilled farm,
where milk and blood blend into the body's moving spark,
where the rains are slow,
where the winds blow an all-consuming message,
and the spinning orbs stop inside the mind's singular eye
Here the light is sucked out of halos that cup the mind and heart
but no darkness ensues, nevertheless.
These dreary paths we walk through
the hands of the water, earth, and air.
They lead us to a place without bliss
and we always seek to be elsewhere
because this is a terrain of woe
but really who knows
that might be where we're meant to be.

A Conversation with God

I think I am an echo lost in a valley of sounds
crashing against the rocks, forever bearing bruises,
floating here like solitary marble hearts in
a saucer of light,
always towards darkness.
The rays pass through my glass self
like rain through the sky's breath,
like the soul moving towards a song

I am an echo hurled between rocky hands, I believe.
But, am I a prayer, or a poem?
Or just a crack through which life falls
and crashes into the soul?
I wonder what the twittering birds
on morning roofs say,
Because the world wears a great veil.
It too speaks in the shadows
and it is okay to not understand
but I listen and listen again.
A flood flows between my ears
and every gurgle is not the sound of sinking
There are days which burst at the hems of my eyes.
There are calls never answered but heard still,
like the pitter-patter of a tropical rain.
Can I listen to the song?
Listen even if I don't reply because maybe I am
an echo not lost or hurled but
held still between the folds
of the universe
coming out of a nebula,
silently, mysteriously
like a bird cracking out of an egg
revealing itself to the light, to us.

HAIKU

A windy seashell
murmurs in the sand's ears
slowly the secret

A drop of rain falls—
the open mouth of the grass blades
closes in the wind

Blood on a thorn dries,
poisoning the stem with
a heavy promise

Clear is the lake—
the crisp ruffle of dry trees,
fog descends low

Flowing floods crash
between the arms
of a broken boat

Silverfish crawl—
an ocean laps in ink
brittle words are tattered

An ant mute, cries
where a hundred cities topple
over her form

Flow steel scissors
cutting the plankton dress
of a still ocean

Flickering sunlight
spreads over the curved sky
A halo at the hems of trees

How restless this world
dark—on its tiptoes falling forever,
forever falling

A leaf wanders on the wind
it spidery soul, past floating trees
the earth slips into dream

A rubble of concrete
catching the wind in its hair
dusty, wiry, stone

These leaves—cut,
sleeping hold their dreams
in a vase of hands

A smell of summer
all the colours of the sun
an unfinished painting and a nail

www.ingramcontent.com/pod-product-compliance
Lightning Source LLC
LaVergne TN
LVHW051703080426
835511LV00017B/2706